This Book Belongs To

_____

Published by Grant Publishing

Sales and Enquires: grantpublishingltd@gmail.com

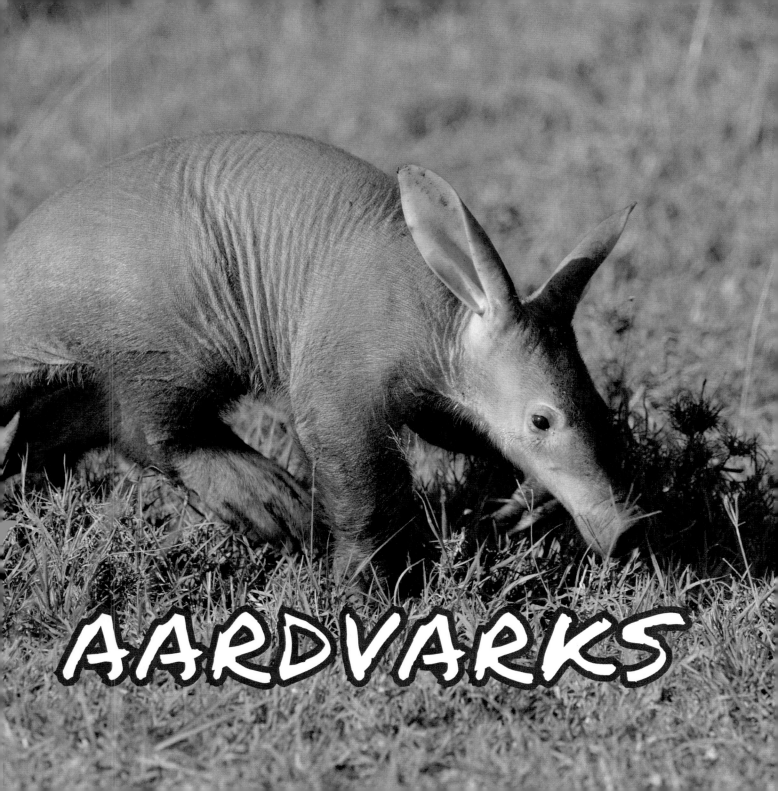

AARDVARKS

Aardvarks are mammals found throughout sub-Saharan Africa.

Aardvarks have long snouts, rabbit–like ears and a tail similar to a kangaroo's

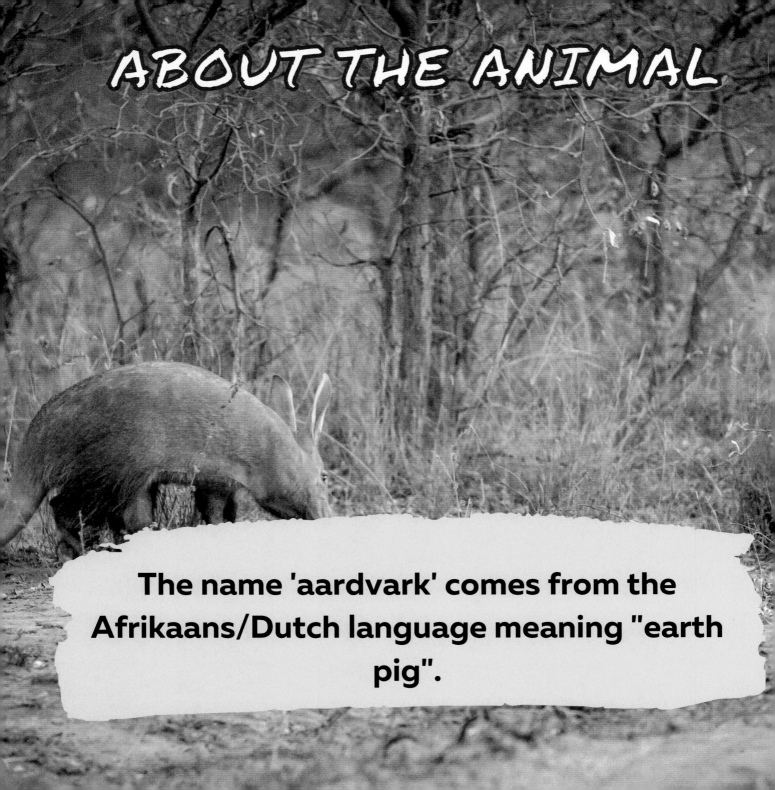

ABOUT THE ANIMAL

The name 'aardvark' comes from the Afrikaans/Dutch language meaning "earth pig".

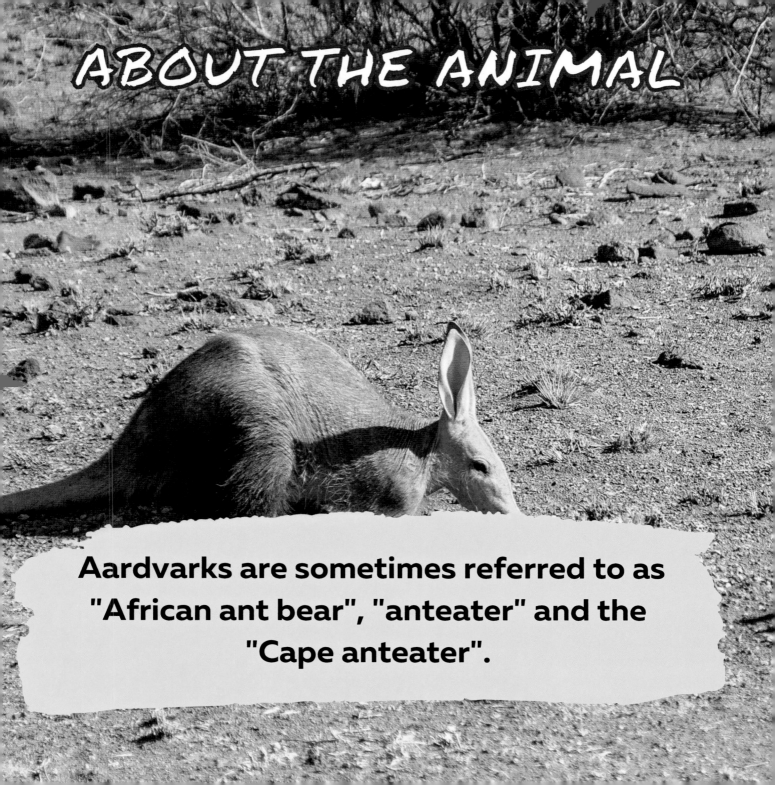

ABOUT THE ANIMAL

Aardvarks are sometimes referred to as "African ant bear", "anteater" and the "Cape anteater".

SPECIES

Aardvarks are the only species in the family Orycteropodidae and the only living member of order Tubulidentata.

SIZE

Aardvarks are about the size of a small pig. Typically, they weigh from 110 to 180 lbs. (50 to 82 kilograms).

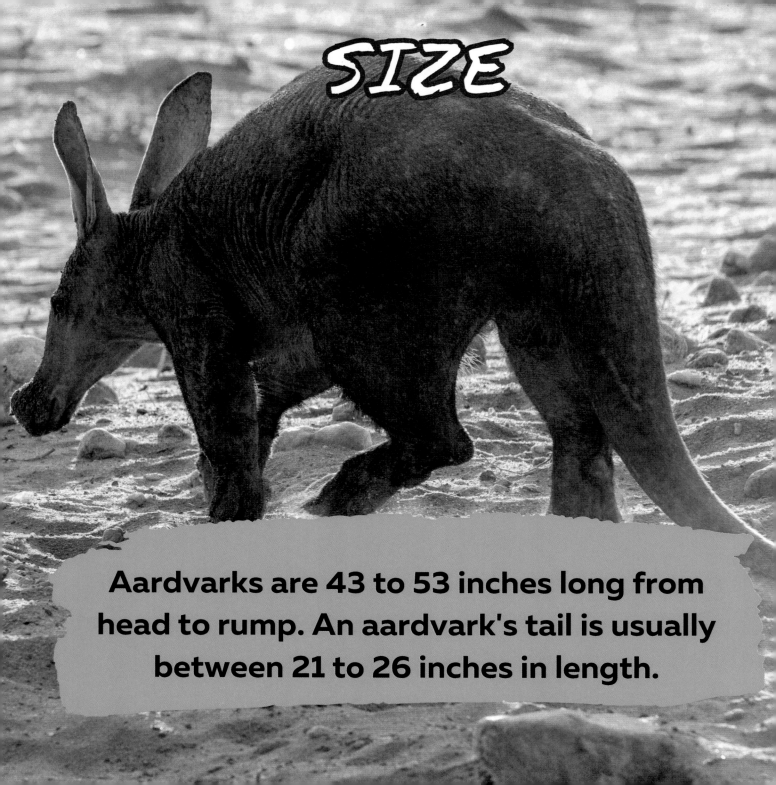

SIZE

Aardvarks are 43 to 53 inches long from head to rump. An aardvark's tail is usually between 21 to 26 inches in length.

WHAT DO THEY LOOK LIKE?

Aardvarks are pale yellowish grey in colour but are often stained reddish-brown by soil.

WHAT DO THEY LOOK LIKE?

Aardvarks have thick tough skin and are covered in a thin coat of hair.

HABITAT

Aardvarks live in a variety of different habitats, such as grasslands, savannas, rainforests, woodlands and thickets.

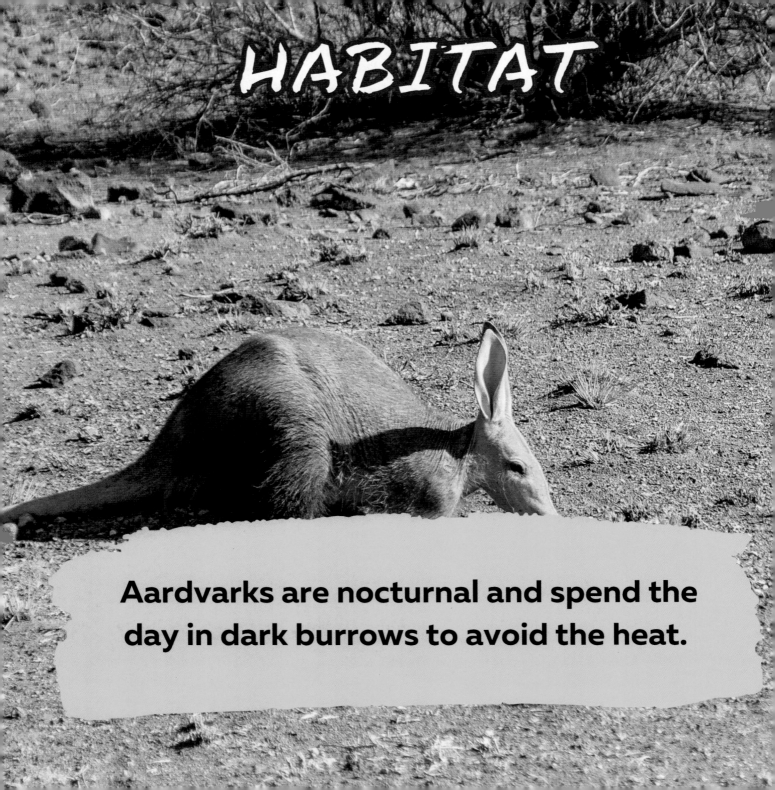

HABITAT

Aardvarks are nocturnal and spend the day in dark burrows to avoid the heat.

DIET

An aardvark's diet almost exclusively consist of ants and termites. It is believed that aardvarks can consume 50,000 insects each night.

LIFESPAN

Aardvarks can live for up to 23 years.

GROUP

A group of aardvarks is called an 'armory' however it is rare to see a group of aardvarks as they are solitary animals.

PREDATORS

Aardvarks are prey to a range of animals such as lions, leopards, hyenas, pythons and hunting dogs.

RANDOM FACTS

Aardvarks have a great sense of hearing which enables them to easily detect predators.

Aardvarks are great swimmers.

Aardvarks are quiet animals.

GLOSSARY

HABITAT

The natural home or environment of an animal, plant, or other organism

PREDATOR

The name given to animals that naturally prey on other animals.

GLOSSARY

PREY

The name given to animals that are hunted and killed by another animal for food.

NOCTURNAL

Word to describe animals that are active/awake during the night.

AFTERWORD

This book gives you a glimpse into the awesome animal that is the aardvark.

We hope that the information provided in this book was insightful and interesting.

There is still so much more to learn about aardvarks. We hope that you continue to learn more about the aardvark and other African animals.

If you enjoyed this book, consider leaving a review and visiting our website www.grantpublishingltd.com for more books.

Thank you for reading

GRANT PUBLISHING